Ten Jolly Jumpers

Written by Judith Nicholls
Illustrated by Stephen Dell

Ten jolly jumpers swinging on the line.

'Let's play,' said the blue one.

Then there were nine.

Nine jolly jumpers swinging by the tree.

'Let's play,' said the red ones.

Then there were three.

Three jolly jumpers swinging in the sun.

'Let's play,' said the puppy.

Ten jolly jumpers
swinging on the line.
'Let's play,' said the blue one.
Then there were nine.

Nine jolly jumpers
swinging by the tree.
'Let's play,' said the red ones.
Then there were three.

Three jolly jumpers
swinging in the sun.
'Let's play,' said the puppy.
Then there were none.

The Snake in the C

Part 1: The Little Sn

The focus in this book is on the split digraphs

'a-e, i-e, o-e' in the words:

lane game cave gate snake

safe wake place came

shade inside woke

Kevin and Lotty were playing by the farmyard gate. Suddenly it swung open. The little dogs ran out of the farmyard and down the lane.

They ran down the lane until they came to the field with the rocks. Kevin took Lotty across the field to the rocks.

The little dogs played on the rocks. They played a jumping game. Soon they were too hot. They went to look for a cool place to sit down.

Lotty flopped on the grass in the shade of the rocks. Kevin was still looking for a good place to sit when he saw a cave.

Kevin took Lotty inside the cave. It was cool. The little dogs lay down and they soon went to sleep.

Suddenly Lotty woke up. She felt cold. She wanted to go out of the cave. She tapped Kevin to wake him up.

'Hiss ... sss.' Oh no! There was a snake in the cave. 'Hiss ... ssss.' Lotty tapped Kevin again. He woke up. He saw the snake too.

Kevin and Lotty were shaking all over. They were scared. They carefully crept past the little snake and ran out of the cave.

They ran across the field to the lane. They ran down the lane to the farmyard. They rushed into the kennel.

At last they felt safe with Wellington in the kennel. They told him all about the snake in the cave, but he did not believe them.

Vowel graphemes used in this book

ay, ai, a-e, a:	playing gate lane came game place shaking shade cave lay wake snake again safe played
ee, ie:	sleep believe field
y, i-e:	by inside
o, o-e:	open over cold told woke
oo:	soon too cool
oo:	took look looking good
ow, ou:	down out about
or:	for
er:	over
ar:	farmyard
are:	scared carefully